NOTHING BUT LIGHT

also by Barbara Schwartz

Any Thriving Root

NOTHING BUT LIGHT

BARBARA SCHWARTZ
& KRISTA J.H. LEAHY
POEMS

CIRCLING RIVERS
RICHMOND, VIRGINIA

Copyright © 2022 Krista J. H. Leahy and Barbara Schwartz

All rights reserved. No part of this book may be reproduced in any form, including electronic, without permission in writing from the author.

CIRCLING RIVERS
PO Box 8291
Richmond, VA 23226 USA

Visit CirclingRivers.com to subscribe to news of our authors and books, including book giveaways. We never share or sell our list.

ISBN: 978-1-939530-23-3 (paper)
Library of Congress Control Number: 2021953452

ISBN: 978-1-939530-24-0 (hardcover)
Library of Congress Control Number: 2022930030

Cover art: Dove No. 2, by Hilma af Klint. Collection of Olomouc Museum of Art, Olomouc, Czechia

Poems in this collection have appeared in the following periodicals, sometimes in different versions:

The Common, "They Say You Are Everywhere" by Krista J.H. Leahy

Denver Quarterly: "Of Two Minds" by Barbara Schwartz & Krista J. H. Leahy

Mayday, "Empress of Ice Cream," "Weeds" by Barbara Schwartz; "Human Sacrifice" by Krista J.H. Leahy

Nimrod International Journal of Poetry and Prose: "Counting Blessings," and "Waking Up" (published as "The Empress"), by Barbara Schwartz

Propertius Press, Spheres and Canticles: An Anthology of Poetry: "The Wax Museum" and "Regeneration," by Barbara Schwartz

For our children

In the beginning, the feminine
principle was seen as the fundamental
cosmic force. All ancient
peoples believed that the world was
created by a female Deity...

— *Judy Chicago*
from "The Dinner Party: From Creation to
Preservation" (2007)

contents

Birthday | 13

I.

They Say You Are Everywhere | 17
Morning & Evening, the First Day | 21
The Living Place | 22
Raw Materials | 25
Whose Arms | 26
Wedding Day | 27
Four Found Subjects from Divinity's Trunk Show | 28
Scrubbing Loneliness | 31
Parable of the Prodigal Daughter | 32
Election Day | 34
Human Sacrifice | 36
How to Grow My Own | 38
Toward and Away | 39

II.

Grafting Evanescence | 43
Tikkun Olam | 46
Of Two Minds | 48
Circling the Garden beside the Angels | 50
Washing Day | 53
The Wreck Is Alive Again | 54
Waterlogged | 56
Empress of Ice Cream | 58
Dressing Up for the Cathedral | 60
Beyond | 62
Air | 63

III.

What Used to Be Called Longing for Angel Wings | 67
Wholewhore | 68
Moanday | 70
The Wax Museum | 71
Rough Draft | 73
Regeneration | 74
The Great Nothing, a Painting | 77
Waking Up | 79
The Hermit, Entrancing Rocks beneath Snow | 80
Counting Blessings | 81
Noday | 84

IV.

Born with Heart Outside Body | 87
Daybed | 88
Garden Birth | 89
Orange Blossom | 91
Honor One Another, or How to Rhyme Orange with Pear | 93
Weeds | 95
Hilma AF Klint's Painting Childhood Writes a Poem | 97
Friend of the Dead | 98
Disappearing Act | 100
An Offering | 102
Air as My Own | 105
Indivisible by Fractions | 106
I Have Missed You All My Life | 108
Daylong | 110
My Kind of Goddess | 111
Someday | 114
Acknowledgments | 115

NOTHING BUT LIGHT

Birthday

Before presence, before sound,
this waning wax candle bears all
time, and a universe —

bang — is born. Inside,
my mother's timeless song.

I.

They Say You Are Everywhere

Through mantle, earth, gender, air
        through false stories and true
undistracted by pectin, pucker, time
        scale, sugar, seed, dripped rainbow of
oil, prism, crushed berry residue,
        om of home, acid, oxygen song —
I grip jelly jars to my eyes
        mock binocular my way to You —

      *

I open a tin of sardines, roll down the lid,
for a moment they look alive, fragrant

        in the oil, I will not eat them, how
        my father loved their salt and bone.

        To love — like all infinitives, free
        from tense and subject.

My brother reads to me, *To gut the trout,*
slit the abdomen, slice off the head.

        Catch without release. Instructions fail
        to prevent intestines spilling into air.

        To catch — like all infinitives, bound
        by form and limit.

My son screams, *I hate salmon!*
His voice uncorks the atmosphere.

        I wish salmon never existed!
        The smell is everywhere!

        To hate — like all infinitives, unlimited

                    utterance facing obsolescence.

Such mermaid hair, my lover teases
as we sun on the deck, topless,

            wet locks and soon-to-be licked
            skin beyond the sight of land.

                    To be — like all infinitives, subject
                    to ebb and rise, evanescence.

                              *

Jelly jar glasses do not help me see or find
            but they reveal how little I
see, how little I find, so blind,
            how dark is our daylight,
ocular oracles blur meaning —
            forgive my ogling, my eye's yodeling,

how else can I believe how much
            I am not seeing

                              *

Ichthys, meaning fish, ubiquitous
Christian symbol — horizontally —
was first a fertility symbol — vertically.

Two curving arcs, crossing,
reminiscent of every woman's
fishy glory and world womb within.

Shape of almond, boat, lemon, eye,
flower, yoni, cry mine newly christa if ever
we meet, pet, nuzzle sap, agree on overlap.

Vertical to horizontal, womb to fish,
female to male — why the flip-flop?
who's the fry chef? How much spin

til we lose our hats? Blow our tops?
Imagine a world-blown pregnancy.
Womb, be fruitful. Sashay the sea.

Mother, sister, friend, daughter,
shake my hips, slake my lips,
slip me moon consort, for our planet too

is round round as breasts, round as
bellies, round as roe, round as berry
go round, all fall down, notes suckling

mouths, mewlings, moonsoothed sea,
school to sleep — Crone wise, Girl wild,
silent Partner, Love Mama, how to pray?

*

Sin-smear my mouth with smash of fruit,
seeding lips with keys of longing —
Knock, unlock, anyone home?

*

Thousand-petaled lotus, blooming in the mud
suggests the spin is perpetual, constant as the sun

each fish a petal, petal an eye, eye a leaf,
leaf a door, door a boat, boat a fish, fish a scale

I could go on but no matter number, name,
reach for a numinous more manifest

I cannot reach infinity, divinity I am
so finite, so limbed, it's hard to wake up

having dreamt of utter beauty strung
as an instrument I cannot describe

beyond hand-hewn uniting of wood and metal,
male and female, forward and backward, fish and scale,

turn and still, pluck and sweep, psalm and palm
aquiver as thumb harp joins finger zither

achieving union in one hand at least
I am only one hand, where is my mate

what is the sound of humanity clapping

I try to strum what does not exist
and the missing music makes me
               (   )

*

My jelly jar glasses expire
from too much longing
colliding with gravity.

I bury the shards in my yard.

Maybe they will grow
into a preserved fruit tree
no one can see.

*

to not-see
the infinitive I am left with

a fish walking out of water

Morning & Evening, the First Day

She said she longed for it,
for church, the way a dog begs
to be let inside when it's pouring out,

when the wind howls back
& the ground rattles underneath
your feet, said she longed for it

the way the sun can't see
its own face, how a shadow's lost
without somebody to follow

home, said she longed for it
the way age makes women ache
to be seen. So she asked her friend

to help her build a church near
the doghouse, in the far corner
of the yard, under an old weeping

willow tree, & the presence
of rain & wind, stars & moon were
co-congregants, co-conspirators

as something vast over-
whelming undeniable washed
over them while speaking the new

testament under the nailed slats,
their bodies supine in the dewy
grass & bones, as love begat

morning & evening, the first day

The Living Place

With reluctance, she obeyed and sent
    her only son up to the mountain.
        The evening hours expanded

    and snapped back like a bow
and arrow when her son's flushed face
rushed through the rambles.

He had returned, and from in his arms,
    jutted a lamb, alive, his black
        eyes fissuring the mountainside.

    Humming the hymn of fallen
        snow and stripped bark, mother and son
            lifted the newborn, praised

        She Who Listens for the motherless
    lamb, She Who kneads barren
bellies. They would sooner eat

bees or drown than tear her flesh
    though they were hungry and growing
        hungrier as the moon swelled

    and shrank. *You must make a sacrifice,*
she heard. Her son was already
12 years-old. His hair had been shorn

many times. Every cell of his
    would age and die to keep
        from dying. Had he not shed

    his absent-minded smile,
  his days consumed by the mystery
of flesh. In defiance she replied:

Haven't I lost them already?

*

She Who Listens knows
my mother is hungry.
We'll starve here. I must
go again and search
the mountainside
for seeds, meat
leaves, Black Birch oil.
Mouse in the raccoon's
mouth, the owl who finds
them both, snatching
himself a double meal —
they're not mine.
We're starving here. I must
search the mountainside
for anything. She Who Listens
knows I must but who will
save this motherless lamb?
How can I leave again

without time passing by?
Time keeps passing by
the way an owl swoops down
and vanishes into the treeline,
how the mouse disappears
inside the raccoon, inside
the owl, inside the branching
twilight. Doubled over I think
I'm disappearing inside myself.
She Who Feeds Me offers only dark
pearls of dirt and sweat. I must
go or I will starve here.

*

>   Up and away from the wolf I flew
>   into the boy's arms, nestled in his shirtfolds, my fleece
>   smoothed over and my ear whispered to.
>   I shall call him
>   He Who Listens.

*

Do you hear the cowbells ringing?
The dull blade along the wood? Knocking
hunger? Do you hear that voice, the one
that shouts out sound? Whorls of white
milkweed floating above and just out of sight?
If you are listening then you know you will
give yourself over, your failing eyes
and swollen tendons, blood and sinew,
body unfurled like a tongue,
for your daughter, your son.

Raw Materials

when I dress as the goddess
I abandon the black fetch of
lace garter and underwire bra
instead await dawn in
soot of midnight starlight
constellating pulse points
sub-throbbed burn, whimpered
gnaw of mouth on knuckle
tendril spiral of tree bark
feathers, light-glinting glyphs
of touch and how, spent, felt
experience of inhale, exhale, grail
made new as skin consecrated
by wind, age, death, birth, lust
acceptance, written word, unspoken
wish all
raw
materials
one-handed unclasp
of my vertebrae *gasp*
all my drawers are spilling out
naked at last I know you now as
I knew you then, divine concert —
sort my senses

Whose Arms

make unmake, stitch unstitch, inhale exhale, plant pull

above my brow, infinity combs blooms
I only lack the wit and appropriate clothes

I will knit myself a torso, corset, linen skin
sacred vestment with a thousand sleeves

for who knows which way divinity's arms
may ask me to move, garden, conceal, grow,

so much repetition, variation, to what end?
only when one is all does the dress not change —

change endlessly if the body is more pain
than you can stand, start smaller — parts closest

to the heart: ribs, nipples, breasts, embrace
release: lover, sister, brother, child, chafed self, silence

sorrow, sacrament, sacrilege until we can bear
the ripped seam gasp of the cloth from which we

pull plant, exhale inhale, unstitch stitch, unmake make

Wedding Day

Calling All Lovers! Come! Wake
the Feminine Divine! Where?
When? How? Why? Which preference,

pleasure, peril? Kiss, tryst — first.
After — who, who, who are you?

*

Beloved men. Accept, embrace
self, size, sex. Enough — more than
strong enough, shoulder enough

to lean on, dream on, bite on,
in the unrestraint of night.

*

New bride, new seed, eternal
fire newly lit by plow, wick
and want, woman, wanton spring

bides Her time, willing to bear
even winter's mask to plunge hot.

Four Found Subjects from Divinity's Trunk Show

Permissions Tree

Inhale pine, macadamia, juniper, palm,
almond, cherry, apple, fig, peach epitome,
          persimmon *permisso*.
branch and twig of blood, stone, story, sea
flesh, yes
          dangling
fruit of rotating constellations,
alphabetic numerals, sachet of DNA,
musical notation, blue felt, outline of spine
each fruit dripping seeds
      You   May   Be   Yourself

Design for Open Phoenix Cage

Love educed
to the creamy moon line
of a hot glue gun.

Twist, curl and glint of wire —
how much fire caught
in form which incandesces
but will not burn.

How the Egyptian Goddess Sekhmet Became a House Cat

Female erotic life force:

A lion caped crown
women wear, borne
as birthright breath
in, out, circled round.

Deemed too potent
for femininity, a roar
requiring access to entirety —
ribs, lungs, organs unbound.

How to make natural
unnatural, quite a trick.

Necessary to strip
majesty, rob hunters'
fierce stealth
of soft paw, hard
claw, jaw capable
of breaking a neck,
of carrying cubs
by scruffy napes, tender
nip, delicious bite of mate.

Feminine reduction:

*Shhhh! No one will love you
if you're that _____.*

*Aw, kitten, don't be _____,
come here pussy pussy.*

I don't think Sekhmet is content.
Her breath can transform fertile land to desert —
barren abundance full of prickly
places that hurt, too much heat,
not much nourishment.

Hard to survive as a feline.
Cavernous crescent mouth.
Hear her purr? *Watch out.*

Old-Timey Revolving Bathroom Doors

Forgive them Father					Teach them Mother
					for
			they			else you damn them to all
							ways be they who

		know			not		what they do

Scrubbing Loneliness

Today's bluebells were ones I did not visit.
Not a mile away there is a whole field humming

bluebells beyond compare. Where is there?
I would rather have been humbled by their

bell blueness ringing racing rumpling free
the field than bowed by problems of the day,

but today had problems, so I bowed. Surest
sign of middle age, Moanday, Winceday, Sunkday

Noday for silliness — today needed bluebells and today
didn't get them, except a lone parched patch, sidewalk

starved. How long years of trial grimace, gasp, practice
calluses instead of tenderness, rubbing cracked heels,

scrubbing loneliness, nowhere and everywhere seeking
a soundbow, crown, clapper to peal that blue, blue mouth.

Parable of the Prodigal Daughter

Dreams of burning her home's bones brought some small solace.
Mostly she smoked American Spirits and watched birds
smash into her window panes. After searching for months,

the mother found only a thumbprint
of the moon. Yet from the kitchen, her daughter's
fallen body emerged: potato eyes, moldy heart

of palm, clock hands, an ex-boyfriend's whiskey mug.
She had the urge to cut something other than herself.
From her neighbor's fields she plucked

yellowed grass to braid hair, acorns for toes, twig hands.
Often the mother could be found kissing the face
of her daughter carved from a single wooden drawer.

It held the scent of baby powder, chocolate-stained
denim, the insole of a boot, cotton from a torn bear.
She forgot to eat, to clean, to breathe. She stole

crows from the air, a mischief of mice from the stairs.
These caged pets formed her child's torso. The legs she left
undone for fear of love's departure. In her dreams

her daughter returned. She wore a stained tunic,
a garland of weeds, responded only to Saint Francine.
A frog curled around her ear, a snake around her arm.

She spoke in palindromes:

> *Madam mom*
> *Tattarrattat.*
> *Sagas solos wow.*
> *I did didn't I?*
> *Step on no pets.*

Bird rib borrow or rob.
Are we not drawn onward, we few
drawn onward to new era?
Cain: a maniac.

The mother felt closer to the cage, the grass, her draw
of memory than this stranger. What happened to the girl who buried
herself in her shirt-folds, shrinking from slugs, voles, the color

of blood? Who was this woman she followed, would follow
onward into the woods each night to count the trees and
breathe the scent of the wind, the wind that ravished everything.

Election Day

Each dead-end seemed to say, yes —
    to the bowed heads of old
        voters and new, to the chosen

        jewels of pigeons and doves,
    to the psalms of blind wind
urging us onward —

Finally, we found a door
    to the Gardens, home to our roped-off
        Walking Crabapple tree.

        Shadows as scarves, bandages, balms
    we offered to her wounded
trunk, all our fevered songs of fall — droplets

clinging to leaves, leaves to boughs. Yes,
    to holding-on-for-dear-life,
        to *One Art*

        replicating itself, just as this
    body reimagined one limb, then another,
sprouting one straight up to the sky

with separate roots
    — a new walking tree! —
        The original bole transformed by eating

        pilgrims of air flitting and glowing there.
    Counted among the supplicants, we bowed
yes to emptiness, to loving everything

that goes wrong. We yearned for her
    scent, her boughs' once pink mouths:

This hollowed out trunk — my death but another

    breath

        somewhere else

Human Sacrifice

Sensei Izzy instructs — look before you move,
you never know what might be behind you —

Wall, enemy, ally, shadow, tree, a toddler
given freedom to roam, requires one

banana-nut muffin, many hands, 56
minutes to walk one Brooklyn city block.

Up close, red hawks seem enormous. But
still not big enough to explain how they

make such bird-shaped holes, scraping
open the sky, teaching us reality. Flying

winged shadows across streets, buildings, forgotten
walls. If I could offer my head to the stars I would.

Not so practical for 2 pm pick up — allies, enemies,
all the other mothers will have their heads attached,

not be bringing starlight as an afterschool snack.
In the condo that belongs to my dead

mother-in-law, a coat rack resembles a tree.
Pyramid sounds like permit if said fast enough.

Is this enough to excuse human sacrifice?
My apologies. Let me pack up the starlight

in the pyramid of my body. So nicely quarried
in my flesh and the tippy top capstone so much

closer to the hawks' descent. Sometimes Sensei,
you must move first, or risk never looking again.

Scraping against a shadow I cannot see, licking
crumbs of what could be called a muffin, if I were

a toddler, if every minute were a year, if my
all, my everything, were but a single beakful of

afterearth snack — awaiting ravishment by
Sensei-to-Wind-and-Trees, I stumble, skin free.

How to Grow My Own

what song unsings us
so we may return
our music to the wide
scroll of non-existence
we have lost so many
of our birthrights
empathy, music, how
to move unheard,
our sense of being
one with the world
our deathrights too
have been misplaced
please, restore all rights lost
unwrong our time signature
teach me my dirge
how to unblossom notes
so when I'm 508
my great-great-great-
great-great-great-
grandchildren grown
I could dignify all
I've done and seen
and said and sighed
with the unmusic
of this is how I lived
now listen how I die
no need to sacrifice
flowers to my grave
hear the dirt turning
and tuning I am
orchestrating how
to grow my own

Toward and Away

The temple's mouth glows with bowls of oranges, crystal chandeliers,
pillars of fire for teeth. Red neon, red apples, red table cloths, red

chairs lined against the walls like soldiers. A girl's stuffed dragon
guards my row of red cushions. Someone bedazzled bows, her white

wig covering her face like a cloud. I keep breathing. A woman
with moon eyes twirls silver balls in her palm. Laughing children spin

down the aisles. One steals an orange from the altar and takes a bite.
I breathe in; I breathe out. Words take me away from my breath. Take me

away. My legs are on fire with neon and light. The Buddha seems to be
smiling as if to say, it's all maya. Did you know the Buddha had a mother

named Queen Maya? I didn't. I'm no longer a girl or a mother but a body
that bows and breathes and does not need to take in every other body,

every other pain or imagined pain and make it mine. What's mine is
an illusion. My son's not mine. He grows with time. My body's no longer

a mine. Yemaya, is time on our side? My jaw unclenches. My ankles
and arches untighten. My neck muscles loosen as the Buddha's two

fingers touch the tops of my knees. I'm watching myself as I breathe.
Am I disintegrating? No. I am red. Bedazzled pillar running

toward the laughing moon. Silver in my palm. Balm. Alms. The bitten
orange, the bite, the rind, the juice, what's left before and after breath.

II.

Grafting Evanescence

Today my friend and I visited a Walking Crabapple Tree,
elder trunk hollowed out as it nurtures its last living branch,
bowed down, rooting in the ground to nourish a new sapling.

1. What happened

I ask, are You absent? Where? Moon? Margin? Arranged marriage?
Malus Floribunda fast asleep? To await a kiss? Dream of afterbirth?
Bloody show of crabapple, torn asunder? On whose authority have you
been split off? Lopped, cropped, silenced? Unmistakable, the hum of you,
please, moisten your lips, open your lungs, dig down past the diaphragm
keeping us too long apart, I want to hear you sing.

2. What might have happened

Like a quarantine (rain splotch washing
out original notation)
sitting inside, remembering outside —

How it feels to miss goddess
...ghostess hostess guestess?

ghost, host, guest share
the same ancient root. *ghos-ti*.
guest-friendship, reciprocal
duties of hospitality (splotch)

Perhaps the ground out there is strewn with fallen crabapples.
In here, wet papers, empty mouths, breaking to our knees,

all we have left are hidden roots —
What might make Her feel at home?

3. What didn't happen but could have

In one original alphabet it is thought
m might be the symbol for water,
n the symbol for snake.

Eve + Adam = Edem
if you alternate every other letter.

How do you take your divinitea, one hump or two?

Eat a fallen crabapple and ponder
the possibility of splitting the garden,
deviling an Atom.

m of may be, *m* of mate, *m* of *mons Veneris*=love.
n of no, *n* of never, *n* of naked=sinfulness.

Why not the wholeness of all?
Why insist on dividing up the world —
why slice your own head into layers?
The heaven of cake means accepting the hell of strata.
Thank you for making that clear, Marie Antoinette,

I want the garden where water welcomes, waves, winds us all
and the one where the snake slithers, sycophants, disappears.

4. What happened before

Marie Antoinette, Marie Curie, Virgin Mary, Mary Magdalena
Mary Queen of Scots *(see Camperdown Elm),* Mary Poppins,
Mary, Mary Quite Contrary, what comes after marry?

5. What happened

If god is not just within, but also the within —
love in love, devotion in devotion, ache in ache —
what if goddess is the *in*. The way *through*.

Relationship itself.
So seeking Her independent of

is like mistaking an echo for a voice

Today my friend and I visited a Walking Crabapple Tree.

The tree walks.
Old to new. Death to life.
Bowed to straight. Hollowed to whole.
Hallowed to (no splotch just space)

The hope is the new roots will be enough to sustain
the young tree when the elder finally dies.

What susurrus is required to let the walking feminine sing?

If one is connected to everything — if One is the connection of
    everything — how confusing
to find so many cuts and wounds, forgotten limbs, disconnection,
    blocked paths.

Please, I invite all to walk *in* what happened.
Walk through me, as I walk through you.

Tikkun Olam

for Rabbi Timoner of Congregation Beth Elohim

We sit in the empty synagogue, taking in the scent
of century-old prayers, a mezzanine, so many scarlet stairs
down to the bimah, and my friend says, *I think I will go
and write,* and I hear her say, *I think I will go and pray.*

    whose home is this?
    the glass is beautiful, stories
    sacred, yet all the natural
    light that enters here is filtered
    by mosaic paeans

Congregants swear they have seen our rabbi cleaning
the sanctuary on her knees, reciting Kaddish,
kissing siddurs in the sapphire hours, scaling a ladder
four times her size to shine the enormous broken organ.

I wade within the many murals: lift squealing Moses
from his wicker basket, drink the opal sky; watch Moses
part the Red Sea, try to save the shadows lost to the depths.
Light spills a small god beside me. He does nothing

    the cleaning man folds the chairs
    reverently, never faster than
    the pace he attends to his own heart
    squeezing drop after drop
    of milk into red-windowed reeds

but reflect upon himself. Did you know that our rabbi
changes each bulb of wrought-iron Jewish star
chandeliers and tiny flickering memorial lights,
by hand? Here in her temple, to davan means to move
and be moved, to tend to her flock, her home
which is as much ours as the domed roof is the sparrow's.

what do you say to us Shekinah?
perhaps you have disrobed language
as a flimsy and distracting
garment like stained
windows for the ears

Does it pain her — how each piece of glass is so fragile,
so easily broken? Yet this fractured arrangement,
the totality, lasts. To the left of the organ it reads,
Have we not all one Father, and I mistake it for *one Mother.*

Of Two Minds

We were chosen
not to be there, at the table,
as the museum and therefore Judy
Chicago's *The Dinner Party* was closed
for voting. I was made to recreate the table
from memory, vulvar in shape, place settings designed,
sewed, fired by women to honor women, some wearing opals
some rags. The table allows for no head, no dominant member,
a continual shifting openness. O, to drink wine from Virginia Woolf's cup
and dine from her plate! Such emptiness! I am not starved for the imaginary;
I want fascia, each textured lip of bowl, rim, tine. Is that my plate of crenellated
purple Columbine? I shall learn how to alternate course intercourse consensually.

Tell me Sojourner, Georgia, Susan B., Virginia:

*G: I feel there is something unexplored
about women that only a woman can explore.
S: If the first woman _____ ever made was strong
enough to turn the world upside down,
these women together ought to be able to turn it right again.
S.B.: Men, their rights, and nothing more; women, their rights, and nothing less.
V: The truth is, I often like women. I like their
unconventionality. I like their completeness.
I like their anonymity.*

What if the meal we make is for ourselves? How to conceive of the whole when
only part has been permitted? What if instead of a last supper we dine at a
perpetual one? Where does the _____ sit at the table? With
whom does she toast? Does she ensure no one feasting is invisible?
Who is the Seer? Who Sees? Untouched plates and bowls appear,
the soundlessness between the cutlery, the sound of round
without saying it aloud. Is She guest invited and excluded,
energetic space co-created by the empty triangle? Why
must she have a body? To dwell among us? Could She
be one of a chair's four legs, splintering from

the weight of all that beauty? Must
a God suffer, hold weight, to be
a God? Might She hold
nothing but light?

Circling the Garden beside the Angels

*Those who are said to learn only remember,
and learning is recollection only.*
— Plato, Phaedo

Metal holes
of the fence expose
a dark green
sculpture garden
for children,
though the giant
fallen angel's wings
and the small starving
herd he tries to nurse
frighten my son.
He decides he wants
to walk inside
with his eyes
closed and touch
the animals up close
but the entrance
is locked. Maybe
the creatures are not
falling but rising
toward some invisible
blue fountain
and we are two stone
supplicants who crane
toward him? Thirsty
we leave and find
St. John the Divine
Cathedral's door,
gulp our juice,
race through pews
to the empty

altar where we spy
new sculptures
of stone children.
*Why are they
carrying dead things?*
My son says aloud.
Each statue holds a fish
with X's in its eyes.
I press him against
the folds of my
jacket and whisper
something into his ear
that makes him grin.
I want to swim again
through waters as
blue as these stained
glass octagons, to be
shaped and reshaped
as when I first
felt him reach
for me, how clear
my breathing became
then and slows now
inside this church.
I'm learning to let go
of my son. I think
of words to express
separation: fenced,
dead, torn, shorn, grown —
They're all partial.
What if the sacred
has always been
cleaved, then
consumed: the cool
water the cool air

coursing through us,
never wholly separate
from the source:
I remember as a child
holding my face
in my hands tasting
the water's salt. The same
salt the same taste that
runs through my hands
as I dry my eyes now.

Washing Day

Did my body need the sand's
weight, Nu's primordial pools
to sense boundaries of the self

as separate though bonded
as molecules of water?

*

If land cannot meet water
on equal terms, sanctity
of self and Gaia, no choice

but mud of unknowingness.
O, how I thirst to be known.

*

Ambergris, what a beauty
of a word for whale vomit,
extending a perfume's life.

I'd brave all insult, even
worship, to divine Her scent.

The Wreck Is Alive Again

The tide's my birthing song —
    Sirens in my veins, deep
        faith in my lungs, I descend

the rope. Deluge of moon jellyfish
    and limbs of blue starfish spiral up
        my thighs: gifts from salty gods.

The drowned boat knows everything:
    the passengers who passed away
        in the doldrums of their dreams,

angelfish who slinked into the severed hull
    to save themselves, this row of faceless
        windows where I float

among the decomposed. My body's not
    mine underwater: it's the voltage
        of the draft, the sun's long sea legs.

Next year or week, I may return
    to the starched white beach
        of hospital sheets, pillows damp

and whispering. Mouths of clams snap
    shut against reeds, and parrotfish boast
        grandiose teeth that cleave

the coral reef. *Will my cells learn to die*
    so I can live? Italics is a pearly keepsake,
        I think, though questions cannot

keep my palms open, up —
    What is prayer but part
        of the mind at rest, the other

ravenous? I stay too long in the depths.
A nurse shark remembers my scent,
circles round again.

Waterlogged

scrape of scale against jaw dredges me from drowning
I cannot breathe, another nightmare of a world
with too much wrong and somewhere the god I cannot find

who needs my love to light his way as he has lit ours —
my skin smarts where the dream scale scraped
me awake, like shaving a non-existent whisker

when my six-year-old notices my stubble
I explain only women who are really wise
grow a few precious wisdom whiskers

would that I were any kind of wise

*

I would grow a beard over my entire body
for you, my love, my god I've never known,
never even wanted to know til now

I hold my own shoulders, arms crisscrossed,
so my sobs will be small
enough my husband will not notice

he loves me but is godlost
and does not approve of what I am longing to do —
pouring my life into the palm of your chest —

here fingers running through your hair,
here nursing in the muslin of night,
here nerves shuddering Christmastime,

until I can swim through these waves,
fit soles flush to pectorals, palms to moss
clavicle, belly to sunken sex, lips

to drowned gills, drink yes please me
drinking you, waterlogged all — heart,
hair, scales entwined, floating free

would that I were any kind of free

*

did you sleep his voice concerned
I never want to sleep again I don't say

didn't dream I shrug, riverwater drying
in my hair, tightening my skin into
daylight, doubt, duality, despair I pray

how can you love us so much yet
not love us quite enough to

and I do not know who I am
asking anymore

Empress of Ice Cream

You are trying to hold on
    to sand as seagulls flit and two crabs
        limp back toward their holes.

    The day gasps its bright
        undoing. I'm trying to talk to you
about sex, what's lost

after marriage, if you believe in god.
    You say you're hungry and
        want some ice cream.

    Behind the sheer curtain
    by the bar, a woman's silhouette:
She swirls her long dark hair,

piles it atop her head,
    then slowly, suddenly completes
        the cones. Strawberry-

        stained fingers, lips, her red halo
    eyes. Night comes on
sticky as milkfat, quick as blood-

wine through teeth.
    I remember yesterday's banquet:
        a pig quartered on a cutting board.

    Her ears perked as if listening
to the whistles as women wandered in
with tanned shoulders,

breasts. Under embroidered cloths,
    scraps of charred flesh fell away between
        legs. I drank my tea with milk

      and thought of the sow
    chained to a stump in the middle
of a graying field. Hunger sneaks up

like two fingers flicking a pink
    succulent moon. I return
      with the top licked off

      your sugar cone. You say
    you believe in this: my mouth on yours
as our soles disappear in the surf.

Dressing Up for the Cathedral

Great Rose Window,
how beautiful you would look
dangling from my giantess ear.

A human-size crucifix
could become my pinky ring.

When growth cannot be measured
in inches, years, wafers, waffling,
how much made, done, witnessed,
felt, helped, hinted, hurt —
Can it really be so simple as how much love
we give? How much love we can bear?

How much is enough?
How can more surpass all?
Where's infinity?

The search the point —
sharp enough to pierce
my other earlobe
from which will dangle
the sun-moon sculpture
from the children's
garden where giraffes
scamper up a spiral
growing as they go
(who cares the measure?)
to the bosom of an angel
strong and kind who looks enough
like the Devil to scare
away the empty swallowing
hunger.

What are demon horns

but inverted mouths
no longer able to eat,
only to gore.

I muse on communion,
munch an Akoustilith tile
peeled off the ceiling.

How many ways to get lost
looking for a way to eat
what cannot be eaten.

*

As I exit the Nave, granite
columns scrape the bare skin
of my feet — a fleshy unwelcome
sound, like a throat cleared
of phlegm amidst silent prayer.
From this sacred space I will carry
two divine earrings, and for a necklace,
I pray for grace — a grass compass
made from what I find missing here.

Beyond

When I die I want to leave behind a relic
for my son: an ancient, once-glittering ornament
hung from a stranger's Christmas tree somewhere.
Though Jewish, I have loved the gospel, its gnostic
mysterious, juiced pomelo fruit: sweet and sour.
Smelling like lemons, my son's hands sour
like baby teeth saved as relics,
or a bit of the umbilical cord, a knowing
path to where the fetal body ornaments
the womb. A path to a life somehow
underground: a survivor grieving
deep in the earth's mantle, not souring
from heat, but like a tardigrade, that knowledge
of space-time, little water bearer, never relic,
alive and mined in the mind as holy ornament.
My grandmother, if alive, would curse any ornament.
Kinehora! My grandfather would shout, he, gnostic
of unspoken pain, who remembered every relic
of his hometown set afire. For eternity somewhere,
for Hashem who did not save my ancestors, I sour
challah with lemon juice so you may know sourness
from me and not from a force beyond.

Air

Sometimes watching ocean tides
I wonder if the earth's
breath condenses into waves

to remind us Someone grieves
for air in these lost days.

III.

What Used to Be Called Longing for Angel Wings

We have lost our sensitivity even to ourselves in the glut in the gut in the gamut of what is our daily assault. So the profane. Sitting by the profane when the sacred has been lost, for if it hits enough to hurt there is feeling left. Abuse as path towards feeling is time-honored and sucks, each repetition leaving you with less sensitivity than what you started with, yet strands you deeper in sensation divorced from feeling and sense.

I hate pornography. Give me the erotic.

Wholewhore

she is mountainous, pendulous
every limb, protuberance, mound of flesh
bigger than the one before and all of it rocking
back and forth, back and forth, rock a bye baby and yes now please
legs open but no need for wide, no need to splay
to encompass the whole world until the whole world comes calling

this pleasure is hers
she seduces no one but herself
she is all of us, male, female, the loveliness in between
we send our daughters here in groups
so they may know themselves, their particular rippled folds, delight in
 their own pleasure, and see how every shape, size, color, contour is
 known, appreciated, beloved
we send our sons here one by one
so they may know themselves, their particular reach and thrust, delight
 in their own pleasure without having to prove they are more than
 anyone but themselves
we send our lovelies here in their preferred configurations
so they may know themselves, their particular individuality, delight in
 their own pleasure, and teach all of us how to know ourselves better

currencies are tolerated only as ornamentation
they are used as fringe on windows, shingles on roof, cobblestone,
 kitchen tile
bills are burnt in offering as often as they are folded into origami boats
 carrying wishes
for those too ill or old or far away to visit the whorehouse

here nothing is sold
everything is given
to those who seek
what might be called wholeness
in a world where an *l* might recall what's been lost
an *r* what's been raped *(all of us)*

come with me to the wholehouse
I will show you the way, then leave you on your own
to discover yourself beautiful irreplaceable adored
so you may (at last, as at first) have the chance
to outrace the shame and violence of our inheritance
and outpant your way into your birthday suit
pant pant pant
until you
explode
newborn
in
breath

Moanday

Three goddesses walk into
a bar. Gaia cries, On the
House! Venus cries, On the bar!

No matter the position,
cries Mary, you'll never score.

*

Freedom-All-Ways proclaims, "Make
as Many Genders as there
are leathers to skin, or tongues

to speak, sup, thrust." Nuts-And-
Bolts nods, "Human or Hyman?"

*

A lover said my breasts
were lopsided: I cupped his balls
like skinless grapes and said: both

small. He disappeared like wine.
Do you like my crooked smile?

The Wax Museum

We can speak and think only of what exists. — Parmenides

Everyone dropped by
to see their ex-lovers

arrayed in the Pantheon
of nude shoulders and hips,

fake grapes spilling
from lips and thighs down

the mirrored halls
of lost causes: adultery,

mendacity, flaccidity, fuzzies.
The curator wooed us

to a chandeliered room.
Without thinking

we posed, our hair pulled
from our faces,

our cheeks buffed,
our hands massaged,

and we fell, gracefully,
into place without

noticing the glittering
signage that displayed

our flaws: this one a bore;
that one a whore.

We remembered
the places, sensations,

where our bodies
were ours, part of a larger

body of aches, mistakes.
Here, the curator said,

*we embody the divine love
of worshipping our dead*

as alive. He nailed a sign
for this year's theme: *Gods,*

polyamorous necrophiles.

Rough Draft

of a poem for the first perpetrator of sexual
violence involving children

He
~~stands alone~~
~~lays bleeding and cold, trussed like a flightless bird~~
~~lays in pieces, hacked into chunks small enough they are no~~
    ~~longer recognizable~~
~~is exiled for eternity~~
~~is exiled for longer than eternity~~
~~is exiled before he was ever born~~
~~is exiled before his father and mother were ever born~~
~~is exiled before his grandfather and grandmother were ever born~~
~~apologizes before he speaks~~
~~apologizes before he breathes~~
~~makes out of his apologies music of such profound beauty, stars~~
    ~~dance new cadenzas~~
~~rips music from his cells~~
~~weeps~~
weeps

and it is not enough

so he begins again

Regeneration

Grass bristled
below   I was maybe
four or five and she
was three Sometimes
I touched her
knee or pressed her
arm and watched
the light tear
the tops of the trees

as we rocked
our legs
intertwined like veins
on a leaf What did she
want Should I have
stopped An ache
like a branch about to
snap A doll's
head dropped
on concrete
Everyone I loved
left The moment
went And went

With my legs
coiled around it
One dusk the town
dog licked my ears
raw, the next
fur sprawled on
Durham Road
Unseeing sparrows
on the swing-set
My neighbor and I
climbed the slide

flew sideways
into pearls of dirt

I don't remember
when our bodies
stopped believing
in gods spring
twigs inchworms
berry juice how
the memory
of our stained skin
turned shameful,
older distant scars
on our wrists

*

Now I want to be held
down during sex
My lover's the spring
breeze, a whiskey-
smooth tongue and
cheek My mind's
the whip

*

I am afraid
that my son
in sadness
in curiosity
in anger will intertwine
with another
in the animal sanctuary
of confusion
only to run away
from himself

the way a worm
leaves behind
half of its body
and grows again

        *

In the ground
time has dug its own
grave and space
is spacious now
So many loves
Fungus bug duff

Roots give more
oxygen than leaves
The planet topless
A giving tree

The children
and their children
walking around
how will they breathe?

The Great Nothing, a Painting

From inside the temple,
a woman says, *Feel the words*
form in your mouth:
lilac, blue, crimson,
vermilion, sepia, indigo.
I do. My tongue performs
sound, sight, touch —
orange, onyx, ecru, yellow.
I look closer. Ten palette
knives appear in the air.
Each colorless,
or with a color I have
never seen before?
Wordless, my mouth
goes numb.

*

In the temple I touch
The Ten Largest. Hilma af Klint
looms larger than her paintings.
The palette knives take on
a life of their own, refusing
her hands, creating their own
heart, a void. I can feel them now,
like words being pulled toward
a black hole. She seems to be
growing smaller. I am thinking:
When I wake up, if I wake up,
how will I describe the colorless?
What is beautiful and painful.
Klimt says, *For years I was full.*
I painted nothing.
My mother was going blind.

*

To describe anything
is to try and describe the divine.

Waking Up

A tarot reader in the dream took one
look at my cards and said, *You are going*

to die. In waking life, I turn over the nine
of swords and every woman leaning

over our long gleaming table gasps.
The tarot reader laughs. *Look closely,*

she says. Yes, a woman carries her head
in her hands. Yes, swords sharpen the dark

walls of her bedroom. But *ever* lives
in *never*. All in walls. You have missed

the life growing from her bed, her cover
of crimson flower, lush buds, that clarity

of yellow. She is waking up. Someone
agrees: *words* hide inside the *swords*.

I turn another card: two women, garlands
in their hair, and a third, each lifting a cup

to the sky, their frocks moving in perpetual
unity. Never have I worn a frock, nor do I

own a golden treasury, and I look ghastly
in orange. Am I awake or asleep? All

the women are laughing now. An *urn*
disappears in *turns*. I am looking, I am

listening. A woman who claims to be
508 years old palms my face, and smiles.

The Hermit, Entrancing Rocks beneath Snow

so carefully
she looks
down, peering
at white-coated
rocky mountaintops
articulating each
titanic toe so
as not to disturb
one flake
of snow light

her staff *Arabidopsis*
grown for waking
mustard, rockcress
dreams of greening
first sidestepping
snow blindness
carnal cacophony —
hush sweep of
white robes, absence
essence

Counting Blessings

Late last night I pulled the Devil
tarot card. That winged beast
    with two naked parents

    chained to his feet. Today,
in the airport our son flails
on the floor, and a stranger appears

with a gift: *There's strength
in being calm,* he says. So I shut
    my eyes and count the chain-

    links still glistening around
our necks. We're attempting
to escape late summer's

wildfires on a red-eye, tears
burning my son's face. Rage
    and Shame can't be counted,

    though they graze, spit. Being hit
in the eye by my two-year-old
moves a crew of teenage boys

to hysterics, and a grandmother
to press open her green eyes
    and bless our heads: *Hashem*

    watch over them. That morning
four years ago, when I woke up
in a hospital with a blood count

of two million platelets, I dreamt
my wrists were shackled to the sun's
    forked tongue, and I missed

      my wedding day, though I did live
a long fiery life. Fear's
my solo star, astrolabe I count on,

just as my husband who kneads
my shoulders as we board
      the plane with our screaming

      child. Fear's the child
I missed carrying, the words
I repeat as gauze to stanch

the bleed. Once I believed
the moon followed me, and
      the waters warmed blue-green

      garlands to warm my neck,
each an exchange against
decay. *It's illusory,* my dad said,

and for years I stopped listening
to my gut. I learned it could not
      be counted on, instead I carried

      our family's bones, their Loss
and Pity like newborn twins
unable to be nursed. My son

sits quietly now, sun waking us all up.
I can't escape. He's buckled in
      with an underwater animal

      book splayed in his lap.
He flails again but this time

he's just pretending to be

an octopus, suckering
his sweet-smelling tentacles
    to my skin, drawing me in.

Noday

I have been trying to talk
to you. What can I do? Show
some skin? Let you in. Beg for

more. I'll close my eyes for good.
My mouth too. Here: will bones do?

IV.

Born with Heart Outside Body

They say, We have put you back together.
They say, You are whole again.

How? How is my heart *in here* and *within me*
when always I feel what is *out there* and *without me*.

Trans: *across, through, on the other side of, beyond*
plant: *to rub, turn, twist, pierce, thresh*

This world, heartless.

Daybed

Achelois whose name means
She who washes away pain,
loofahs my body dry. Now

my thighs chafe a bloodless
tune. My sex, an ancient ruin.

*

Calling all midwives, alive
or dead, labor is about
to transition, chain into

garland, taratantara
into *dulce melos* branch.

Garden Birth

The divine gardener here,
trailing weeping vines past the floor.
When I ask if this place is closed,
she answers, *yes, my name is Rosa,*
all are welcome here, and you two
my dears, may stay as long as you dare.

I love open. I love hello. I love no-name
for walls that hold. I'm off to scaffold
vines so any bud may climb in, up, out.

Behind me, a floral pastoral wall-
paper peels. The birds
are naked and they know it.

*

Am I another gardener within
these walls or do they reside
within me, papery, peeling,
without boundary? Who said

the Garden should be walled off
from the world? What flower thrives
without soil and water flowing from every
outstretched sea? What bird sings
without air that once stormed
clouds there, here, vapor, weeping
rains and nights?

*

Watch me plant morning dew. I want you
to see every move. And if you can't see,
then come touch my hands as I prepare
the earth to be revealed in mundane

mystery. Learn and listen, smell and feel, this
world blooms when you recall all glistens
within you — soft, firm, muscle, curve —
and if you don't like the word for wall —
my love, use your tongue like I taught you to.

*

What grows from me, from my mouth,
it hurts, this vine, it's quick, it keeps
coming and coming, and I can't
stop it, this growing and twining,
pulling my insides out, so I may
eat from the fruit, this fruit, here
pulsing beside me. I take a bite,

and another. What can I see and touch
now that the roots and wings and light
from the moths' wings reside within
my cavity, my fertile grave agape,
with blood and bones sewing this
expanding body I call my own?

*

Bring us water! Bring us blood!
Bring us death, and absinthe tea!
I want my love to see every shade of green
luminosity she is, becomes, regrets, renews.

She's birthing the wildest freest darkest forest ever
dreamed and I want her to have everything
and all, nothing and undone, the letter before
A past the 6th letter after Z. Please,
I'll give her every last drop of me! Or I'll take
her drops and make moondrop stew, something
hearty, effervescent, stinky, wholly new.

Orange Blossom

The sign says Noble Silence.
    The recording chants endlessly.
        Not all silences are the same.
            Three chandeliers of many worlds,

      two descend into my hand
        with the giant gold Buddha as my witness
      (like him, I ask the earth to witness too)
my vow to love in every language

I can learn, knowing that love
    is perhaps not the easiest
        path to the middle way.
            Corona of fire, his expression

        more mischievous and less
      certain than I imagine serene.
    Yellow tulips, mounded oranges
fire extinguisher — not

all flowers fruit, some
    silences enflame.
        I am dizzy viewing him —
            lack of perspective, mine

        shifting eyes from chandelier skies
      to adjacent drums framing
    stage, altar. If, always
the true altar is within,

how do we wake to our
    inner circle, our inner earth
        of offering/altar
            supplicant/communion.

        The story says he stopped
      all killing yet the temple
   is dripping with red.
I am not enough

to understand these circles
    but I bow to the wisdom,
       devotion here. I came
          by subway. I leave

            by rustled scale of green-
        tipped Chinese dragon
fire breathing slow growth.
Shadows move as I write.

He made four bowls into one
    but how many bowls does
        the world hold? The chant
           circles endlessly. Will it wait

            for me to join? Will it permit me
        to leave? Someone, somewhere, alive
    right now must be slowing
shadows, if not stopping them.

noble blossom noble blossom noble blossom

Orange seeds are hidden everywhere.

Honor One Another, or How to Rhyme Orange with Pear

I want to rhyme orange with pear,
delicious with double dare,
honor with utterly rare,
macadamia with that's not fair,
that's not rhyming orange with pear.
Squeeze me an orange forged in the fire,
give me extra vitamin C, plenty of Do Re Mi,
whisper to me your favorite fruit
and I'll whisper back a pair.
Does the fire need more stoking,
or is there enough somewhere heat
to burst an orange into blossom
fleshed, wet, gorgeousness?
I can add some kindling to the flame
simmer your desire, cleanse your shame

How I want to woo the wildness of you

*

Manna from Heaven, Mother's Milk and Justice
of the Peace walked into a bar, ordered champagne
for everyone. The bartender asked the occasion.
Manna from Heaven said, "We were just married
by Justice of the Peace and since there's no justice
and no peace, we realized there was no marriage--
so we're here looking for a date."

Justice of the Peace said, "Where's your honor?"
"Honor?" said Mother's Milk, "We've had enough
On Her for a while, how about some On Him?"

*

Do you want measurements for
honor? A cup of touch, pint of love,

quart of respect, colossus of trust?
Clearly not enough, how about a world
of touch, gargantuan of love, tornado of respect,
bedlam of trust? Might that be enough
to honor you with orange blossoms
falling, calling, cradling your skin
twined with bloom of pear, a sight
not seen too often, bearing wonder
from whimsical to solemn
sidestepping the problem of

How I want to woo the wildness of you

*

I'll endure whatever it takes — rehabilitate,
ameliorate, educate, facilitate, venerate,
exultate — oops that doesn't exist yet.
I didn't mean to language-make
before we had a chance to acquaint —
to pair hands, pair ribs, pair lips, pair hips
paring, we'll forage orange adoring
soon to-be roaring, overflowing,
pouring into where I meet you —
how does this go? Language of me, language of you
isn't that a language of two?

How I want you to woo the wildness of me

*

When I say I dreamt you, I mean I dream
When I say I felt you, I mean I feel
When I say I want you, I mean I want to be
freer than this world has let me be

Weeds

Do you talk to yourself
with compassion? No. It's a chopped-
down forest in here
with axes dressed in worms' clothes wriggling through once-whole
hands. Slice.

Gutted burl. Stupid girl.
Are you listening? I keep talking
to myself with the mauled tenacity of phlox: You will live,
you will rise,
shooting past tree roots, flash

of purple petals despite toddler palms
whose leaves they mangle; the foot of a sot
too enthralled
with Boones and butts to step aside the high
mid-summer shine.

I once saw a girl standing watch over a pageant
of weeds. *Save the flowers!* she yelled.
I think I am my savior's thoughts, the stubborn beautiful ones
who refuse to go. It's a temple in here
though I do not know

the prayers. Ganesha trumpets his long trunk, curls infinities
round my waist. I shrink
in his grace. My neighbor Bina says, *Fix yourself
to what you believe in, center yourself on Him.*
In here God wants to be

a woman. See her flaunting rage red as Kali's tongue.
Rage makes me small, numb
as burnt taste buds. I keep talking
here in the dumb hope that words can turn
to flesh. Here in my ear is Sita burning burning

lotus incense, sensate mother-love, skin-to-skin
teaching. Her arms round
mine lined with off-rhymes: Sadness. Sickness. Hopeless Chorus.
Worthless. Less. Less of yourself. No.
If you are still listening, forgive me.

Hilma AF Klint's Painting Childhood Writes a Poem

The image escapes in every direction.
— Gershom Scholem

yellow tendrils beg
to be plucked off
canvas they
anticipate more
dimensionality
newly born
pistil
or stamen
both bow
to intuition
guardian temple
within built
breath by brush
stroke

Friend of the Dead

The Shaman said he preferred to work in converse sneakers. I made a bad joke about conversing with the divine as he pulled out his oblong leather bag of stones and shook them for a long time. As long as the mouth takes to grind its teeth, to rhyme time: Chime. Climb. Moonshine. Crime. Sublime. Mine. Pantomime. I told him I didn't believe in linear time. He chuckled and stared at the blind stones now strewn on the ground.

The stones said to listen to the Primordial Mother, that blue and white were first her colors, not the virgin Mary's. They stole our mother, he said. The white man stole our healing songs and birthing stories. The wind and rain and stars — monetized. My body, yours.

So, tell me, he said, What has been stolen from you?

I didn't answer. I didn't know. But he kept repeating the question and tapping one finger on his long robe. The tap felt like a boulder rolling down my breasts. Fireflies in the head. A hollowing out for light. Then he told me a story: A woman went on a hike and at the top of a hill she turned to find herself beside a bear. She did everything right: made herself as large as possible with arms outstretched above her head, looked him in the eyes, and waited. She walked backward slowly, her hands gripping her arms, every muscle waking up, until she was far enough away from the bear's mouth.

Aloud, she said, *I am safe. I am safe.*
And even if I was torn apart and eaten by the bear I would still be safe.

Do you see, he asked, this is what has been stolen from you. We sat there like mountains in the sunshine as he touched my streaming face.

I climbed onto his table under a healing cloth of brown and neon pink yellow green threads, the songs of the healing women, he said. But all I could see were the cow skulls on the shelves and his drum held high above my chest. I closed my eyes in the electric blue, and from somewhere, my grandmother's voice: *Yitgadal v'yitkadash sh'mei raba.* She was dead but her voice was not. *Hello my darling. Hello my darling,* she said, dressed in bright sea water robes, and I was small and unable to speak. Her arms her hands her blue velvet skin said, *Everything I am and everything I have is yours.* When I awoke the shaman told me about the friend of the dead.

The next day I fell ill. Everywhere I went in my dreams I found her. The wood of the sauna, the smell of oak and cinder, bright red lipstick, a gold headdress, blue-green garment of sky. Everywhere the bear wrapped around me, nowhere streaming time.

Disappearing Act

On chemo, I dream
more: I see my blood cells rise —

*

My son spots a cardinal
overhead. Trying to say
red, he says, *lead.*
The bird speeds past,
crashes into glass.

*

Hello, Ms. Emily,
Is this the Hour of Lead?

*

*Scarlet, vermilion,
crimson, ruby,
cherry, cerise,
carmine, wine,
coral, cochineal,
rose, maroon,
damask,*

*

sanguine,
a slow
drip.

*

Memorial Sloan's walls
vibrant peony head
without stem; stent of sun;
floating wren's wing
clipped by the frame's corner.

*

I have always envied
Modigliani necks,
their infinite migration.
My trip has been stopped short.
My flock, a hallway of bones.

*

The tiny stuffed bear
that peeks from my purse
is missing an eye. I ask,
Are you a nobody, too?

*

Last night, I read to my son:
Good night moon. Good night air.
Good night nobody. He laughed
as I tried to make myself
disappear.

*

In the waiting room, I see
a statue in memoriam:
Countenance of a bloodless
goddess. Her name is Barbara.

*

Frida Kahlo used her old
gauze corsets as canvas.
My blood has dried out.
I write with air.

An Offering

Latifah handed me a scarf and its blue flowers
blossomed around my hair and shoulders.

Peanut shells gleamed on a paper plate.
You snuck up and tried to reach for one —

Coming to pray, a man smiled at us
and disappeared into the holy place,

empty but for light pouring through
the great dome and walls of windows.

Where the women pray is smaller,
elevated in the air, closer to the dome.

From that height, we saw his bright soles,
his starched white thobe, and searched

for words we understood. Soon more
men crowded below, and around us

mothers streamed in for Salah, laying out
their sajjādāt, guiding their little ones.

We bowed with them, knowing we were all
offering our bodies as offering —

We have always been told to cover
our skin, women more than men.

The children free to be as they are,
dressed in sky and sun and soil's sprigs.

Look! The seed has its seed covering;
the roots their mycelial web; the loam,

every creature's fine-print; water, its gown
of ink and indigo; the turtle, its algal armor.

My thighs and arms, their aging beauty marks.
The day sheds its pale veil for night-cover

and the grave beholds what cannot be held.
I did not give birth to you; I multiplied

malignant cells that would not die. During Salah,
I remember your great-grandmother: her bones

shrouded in linen, her sister's bones lost
to the Shoah. I am named after her, Bilah.

During Salah, I remember your birth
mother, half-blanketed and shivering,

swaddling you. A name covers the body, too.
Your Hebrew name, Shai, means gift.

The more names, the more protection
against forgetting. How do we keep

the invisible alive? How do we keep it
holy? I watch as you bend your body

over the balcony to catch the light, making
wide shadow wings with your arms,

your hands as large as the wall of windows.
When you bow, you make yourself small

again. How the highest mountains were once

something else: low places. From the low place,

here, our bellies press to our knees, our brows,
arms, and hands garden the prayer rugs;

our scent and skin, the plea within; our living body,
a story we have been told and will tell again.

Air as My Own

— for Samuel Lewis,
Sufi Murshid and Zen Master,
creator of the Dances of Universal Peace

There is no reality except the oneness

In the circle of dance, I see the farthest
faces most clearly, and those
closest, whose hands I hold,
barely. How then may I see —

*

At our own pace we begin to spin

I am the maple sap
untapped and sweet

We face our partners and spin together

I am gasp and grass-stains,
branch and spreading roots

We stand still and cover our eyes

Beloved, I am wanted
and unknown. Peel me
and let the stripped bark burn

*

myself? Across the divide
in the eyes of someone else —
Branching as a tree I breathe her
air as my own

Indivisible by Fractions

Beneath the minaret, walls
of avocado green, splash of
newborn blush, tapestry
of the Ka'bah, descending
birdcage of lights open to
the bottom where men
worship —

I divide myself
into 9/10 masculine
and 1/10 feminine
as no more than 802
are allowed to worship
and there is only space
allotted for 78 women —

In child's pose, I pray —

                9/10 of me praises
      Allah's greatness. 1/10 of me wonders
         how God can be He
             and have no partner. 9/10 of me prays
                from beneath the descending lights, aware
        of the circular cordon gracing my life. 1/10 of me
    prays from a balcony mid-way up the mosque, aware
        of how the illumination resembles a cage. 9/10 of me is grateful
for how clean the center is. 1/10 of me coughs at the smell of citrus bleach,
            wondering whose lungs inhale the most
                fumes. Latifah, our generous guide, says
                    "everyone is welcome here"

and I am whole again as 9/10
of my elevated body descends,
1/10 of my body rises from child's pose,
and I walk out, first the sisters' entrance,

then the brothers' entrance to find my friend.

We hold hands, give thanks, wholly of holies —

The entire time we witnessed
the loudspeaker system was on —

yet only static, indivisible by faction.

*

I pray I beg I solicit I sleep
I sing I speak I beseech
1/10, 9/10, 5 times a day,
every hour on the hour —

I listen
for your voice

I Have Missed You All My Life

The Khuya Rumi are unique stones that naturally possess healing energy or have been awakened . . . to enlist their help in healing the beings of this physical world.
— Shaman's Tent

sing me a song of shamans, Khuya Rumi

enter the full room
open the windows to the sky
let fly out what you most need
to release, let fly in what you
most need to receive

sing me a song of stone, Khuya Rumi

ossified feather of strawberry,
red-crested woodpecker, dusty
blood healing stone

with a punched-open heart
I live this life all alone
to mate make matter

would you cross
the circle of pain
into pleasure, when, what is
sense, sensation?

is the universe cold, empty,
worse than faithless,
unfaithful in its brilliant birthing beauty?

*

resin, sage, palo santo
eagle feathers, pull of taffy,

back to my body, the taffy my flesh

I burn and burn and burn, howl
how I want to hew to open-hearted
open-throated open-feathered belovedness

I am no Rumi, but here I sing
to the glimpse I peeked through you

*how now if you want me to forget
you must cut my cucina strings
hope you can outrun my wings*

*

*(yes, for you, beloved beyond
beloved, I would always
forget, if —
you ask*

*please
do not ask)*

Daylong

Yggdrasil at the sex shop:
axle tree atop giant
Redwood, dual gyration,

ancient twist, shimmy, sigh, slide
pleasure old as new as yes.

*

I miss how You poured honey
starlight into my skull, down
my spine hot and all the while

the other restaurant goers
saw me drinking lemonade.

*

More than sensory, prayer
rings a clapper unheard, seen
in bowed head, pressed palms, kneeling

its own bell if you know how
to unlisten – silent peal.

*

All alone within caress
of air, how grateful to live
in skin. Skinned by desire, I

seek more than our physical
loneliness incarnate. You?

My Kind of Goddess

crabapple leaf, clear sky, milky way

come to me any way you wish
brother, sister, child,
lover, parent, friend

what matters the temporary
habit of skin and bones?

I am love
energy, the impossible
unfossilizing
feathers touch and tease

let me dream you being stretched
not the nightmare of knock and rack
the musts, the shoulds, the unforgivables

not the carousel fair of easy dreams, so much sound,
so much spin, too much sugar spun into clouds
windkissed will-o-wisp of anything-you-want-dear

let me dream you the bed of not-quite-nails
prickle of possible, but no puncture, no bleed
the undeniable pulse of what you and only you must heed

separation from divine may be an illusion
but you are here to learn how to separate
from what you think of as yourself

you are not the shell, beloved
even though you might need it to live

you are nakedness within

imagine your bed as the ground
how you are always sleepwalking
in this dream of dust and death
reverie required so we might make new love

new love
what shouldn't be possible
can't be accounted for
balances the equation unbalanced
births an original horizon line

I serve new love in you:

ligament into longing, muscle
to movement, heart to hope,
will you, won't you wander
or wake, wake, beloved
with you I will go so slowly
so gently, with so much laughter
you won't even notice
love pulsing fingertips, leaves,
earlobes, undiscovered globes
over, under, akin, besides, where, when
all ways
I serve you

I am the mother crabapple tree,
where you walk, I walk, where you weep,
I weep, where you sour, I sour,
where you thrive
I bloom into life.

Here, take my body as your root.
Grow a new love might-be-tree.

all over
all under
all wheres
all whens
all ways
I serve you

growing up I was sister
then I was everyone's mother
now I'm everyone's lover
I serve you

Yes, You
could be my kind
of goddess too

Someday

Spring is born of winter's sleep, and sleep from waking
life. So too, do roots arise from wounds, opening
the loam's womb. Rot grows up. Sapling
graves, green us.

*

The weeping tree sees us beside the stream
reaching for Her strands of woven hair.
Braiding ourselves we keep
reaching higher higher
and we catch only
blind sky.

Acknowledgments

We wish to thank our editor Jean Huets at Circling Rivers, for believing in this book and bringing it into the world. Thank you to Kathleen Ossip, our wonderful teacher, whose class inspired the writing of this book. Unending thanks to Joe Pan, Daniel Borzutsky, and Rachel Galvin for their generosity and support. Much gratitude to the Brooklyn Botanic Garden, Congregation Beth Elohim, Brooklyn Museum, Cathedral of St. John the Divine, the Guggenheim Museum, Islamic Cultural Center of New York, Mahayana Temple Buddhist Association, the Universal Dances of Peace, Dina Berrin, Adam Kane, Alvaro Romao, and Judy Chicago.

Krista would like to thank everyone who has believed in her poetry–every member of her beloved book club, her NYU cohorts, Odyssey folk, UW cronies, VSC kindred, Hannah Gersen, Jen Acker, Mike DeLuca, Holly Friesen, Jon Samson, Ken Hebson, Preston Lane, Khahtee Turner, and her entire sprawling, wonderful, incredibly supportive family—both the one into which she was born and the one into which she married. Heartfelt thanks to all of her teachers—not just the poets—most especially to Brenda Shaughnessy. With thanks to Matthew Fox for his book *Naming the Unnameable* which was a source of inspiration. To Banff and Vermont Studio Center for the gift of time. To her friend Michiko, who has always believed, thanks to the moon and beyond. To her aunt Elizabeth, thanks beyond thanks for always welcoming the words. To her mother Margaret, there are not enough ways to say thank you. To her devoted husband Jay, thank you for the gifts of love, belief, courage and patience. To Augie and Sinclair, for so much love. To Barbara, what next?

Barbara would like to thank all of her teachers from the 92 Street Y, Brooklyn Poets, University of Miami, Fordham University, and Sarah Lawrence College, in particular Diane Thiel and Suzanne Gardinier. Eternal gratitude to Komal

Mathew for your wisdom, patience, and faith. Elizabeth Devlin, Christine Gardiner, and Emily Moore—thank you for your witch wivery and unyielding support of these poems. Beloved family and friends, thank you for a lifetime of loyalty and generosity. Much love to Michael for every poem you have listened to while driving in traffic, for every word of encouragement during times of doubt. Preston, little muse, thank you for being you. And to Krista, let us continue the journey inward.